A STEP-BY CHILDREN'S GUIDE TO DOG TRAINING

DENISE P. CHERRY

Photography by Denise P. Cherry, Isabelle Français, Joe Hartnagle, Susan Miller, Robert Pearcy, Ron Reagan, Scott Rowe and Vince Serbin.

Humorous drawings by Andrew Prendimano.

Title page: Saint Bernard puppies grow up to be very big dogs. Soon they will be bigger than their keepers.

©Copyright 1993 by T.F.H. Publications, Inc.

Distributed in the UNITED STATES to the Pet Trade by T.F.H. Publications, Inc., One T.F.H. Plaza, Neptune City, NJ 07753; distributed in the UNITED STATES to the Bookstore and Library Trade by National Book Network, Inc. 4720 Boston Way, Lanham MD 20706; in CANADA to the Pet Trade by H & L Pet Supplies Inc., 27 Kingston Crescent, Kitchener, Ontario N2B 2T6; Rolf C. Hagen Ltd., 3225 Sartelon Street, Montreal 382 Quebec; in CANADA to the Book Trade by Macmillan of Canada (A Division of Canada Publishing Corporation), 164 Commander Boulevard, Agincourt, Ontario M1S 3C7; in ENGLAND by T.F.H. Publications, PO Box 15, Waterlooville PO7 6BQ; in AUSTRALIA AND THE SOUTH PACIFIC by T.F.H. (Australia), Pty. Ltd., Box 149, Brookvale 2100 N.S.W., Australia; in NEW ZEALAND by Brooklands Aquarium Ltd., 5 McGiven Drive, New Plymouth, RD1 New Zealand; in the PHILIPPINES by Bio-Research, 5 Lippay Street, San Lorenzo Village, Makati, Rizal; in SOUTH AFRICA by Multipet Pty. Ltd., P.O. Box 35347, Northway, 4065, South Africa. Published by T.F.H. Publications, Inc. Manufactured in the United States of America by T.F.H. Publications, Inc.

Contents

This illustrated guide is intended for children who are new dog owners. The ownership of a puppy is an enlightening experience for anyone who is not acquainted with the day to day activities of a puppy's life.

The special bond between a child and a pup can stimulate learning, growth, and responsibility which will benefit the child throughout life.

FOREWORD FOR PARENTS

Caring about the well-being of a living animal enriches and stimulates all those who have contact with it. Family members who help support a child in learning to care for a pet also share in the love and respect exchanged between the child and pup.

The parent should know that having a puppy in the house is almost like having another child; but, the time spent in teaching a new puppy is much less, and the results are seen in a much shorter time. The guidance and understanding that the child receives while raising a pup is a valuable part of the growing process.

Consistency is important in training the dog. The puppy will be learning the rules of his new home; the child must therefore be taught what will be acceptable in the new puppy's behavior and train the pup accordingly.

All children need love and acceptance and a puppy can be the ideal playmate. With just a wag of the tail your puppy can make your child smile.

The puppy will be mature in a very short time; the time spent on early training will ensure a calm, well-trained animal that will be a pleasure to have in your home.

FACING PAGE:
As this Great Pyrenees illustrates, growing up with a dog offers a child a bounty of ineffable benefits. Parents acknowledge that dog ownership reinforces a child's sense of responsibility, and provides an example of unqualified affection and companionship.

Oh, boy! Your own dog! Now you have a friend to play with, one that licks your face and shows you that he loves you. Your new puppy is a lot of fun and is also a part of your family. Everyone in the family will want your puppy to be a good puppy and a good dog.

INTRODUCTION

While your puppy is young (six or eight weeks old) you can begin to train him in lessons that he will remember for the rest of his life. This book will show you how to train your dog right and make him a welcomed part of your family.

Dog training can begin as soon as you bring your puppy home. Some things are easy for a puppy to learn. It is better to start training your puppy when he is young. The lessons your dog learns as a puppy will help him later in his life.

Let everyone in your family know the things you are doing to teach your puppy so that no one will show him the wrong thing. Remember, your puppy needs to hear the same lessons over and over again to learn the right way.

The puppy is still a baby in many ways. Make sure you let him sleep because he will often be tired after just a little playing.

In this book I will call the puppy "Tuffy." I am sure you will think of a good name for your own puppy. A name that is easy to say is best. Your puppy will learn a lot of words and it will make it easier if his name is easy.

HOUSEBREAKING

When your puppy is six or eight weeks old it has reached the best age to start the potty training. This training will work on older dogs also, but it is best to train them when they are young; do not housebreak at the same time you train your dog to heel and sit. Too many lessons are not good for your dog. He can only learn a little at a time.

FACING PAGE:
Dogs and kids get along great! This pretty dog is from Japan and is called the Shiba Inu (that means "small dog" in Japanese).

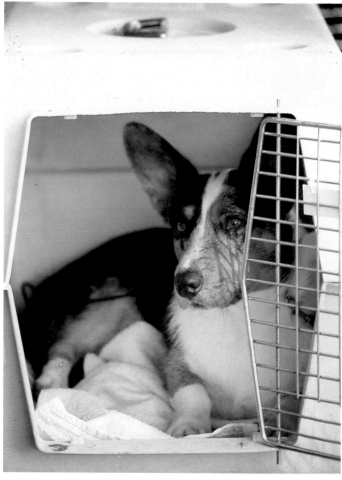

Use a crate to help teach your dog not to piddle in the house. This Welsh Corgi has learned by using a crate.

Even if you do not plan on keeping your dog in your house, you should train him to stay in a crate for travel. The crate makes it easy to housebreak your dog. The crate for your puppy must be tall enough for him to stand up. You want your dog to feel safe and cozy in his crate. It should be only large enough for him to sleep in. There is a reason for this: dogs do not like to sleep in the same place they use for a bathroom.

INTRODUCTION

It is best to have mom or dad buy a dog crate at your local pet store. Your puppy will be growing rapidly; if you plan on using the same crate when the puppy is older, buy a large one, so he'll fit in when he's grown. A crate does not cost very much. It is best to get a new one to protect from any diseases which may be found in a used crate.

At night, put your puppy in his crate with a towel or old blanket on the bottom. The bed should be cleaned each night. If your puppy makes

A travel crate is handy for both housebreaking and transporting the dog to shows and the veterinarian's office. Photo courtesy Rolf C. Hagen.

a mess in his bed you must clean it out right away. He should not think that his bed is his bathroom.

The first week is very important. Housebreaking can be done pretty fast if you have a smart dog and if you do not let him make too many mistakes.

On the first day of house training you will show him the place that you want him to use for a bathroom. This is the place he will always use, so make sure that it is not a place where everyone will walk. If you are going to train him to go on paper, try to put the paper near the door. Then later you can train him to go outside by moving the paper to the other side of the door, and then outdoors.

As soon as your puppy eats his food, take him to his bathroom spot and wait until he uses it. Say "Good boy," and sound very happy.

There are four times that you must take your puppy to his

bathroom spot right away. One is as soon as he eats. Two is when he wakes up from sleeping (night or day). Three is when he has been playing; and four is when he is running around in circles sniffing the floor.

Each hour you should take your puppy outside or to his bathroom spot, even if he does not do anything each time.

If your puppy makes a mistake in the house do *not* hit him. Gently pick him up and say "No! No!" Sound *very* angry at him. Take him outside right away. Then soak up or pick up his mess with a piece of newspaper and put it in his bathroom spot outside. Clean up the accident with soapy water and then put some vinegar and water on the spot. Puppies will go back to the same spot that they used before and the smell of the vinegar will make them think again. They do not like that smell.

Each time he makes a mess in the house do the same thing. If you are careful, you should have to clean up a mess only one time. Puppies do not like to make you angry. They like to know that you are happy when they use their spot outside.

A happy Newfoundland puppy kisses his new owner.

Puppies must be taken outside one hour after their supper. This Chow Chow puppy will need to go out in a little while.

If you have a puppy that forgets and makes too many messes in the house, do not be too angry. Just take him out more often. Remember not to throw your puppy down; put him down carefully. At this age, a puppy's bones are not as strong as those of a full grown dog. They can break easily if the pup is suddenly dropped to the ground.

At night you can feed your puppy about an hour before you go to bed. Then take your puppy out to his bathroom. Do not give him water before bedtime. This will help him to wait until morning to go out.

When you put him in his crate on a towel or blanket you can give him a chew toy to keep him quiet. Make sure that it is not too little or he might get it caught in his mouth. A Nylabone® that is made for puppies is the best. Puppies need to chew to help their teeth grow in; teach your puppy the right things to chew. Do not let him chew on chair legs or bed covers. Even if you think it is cute for him to pull on the curtains, this is not right.

Your puppy needs to learn the rules of your house. Even if you think something is cute for him to do, someone else may not like it and get angry.

When your puppy is in his crate at night, do not feel sorry for him

Remember that your puppy has just left his brothers and sisters. You are taking over as the puppy's new family member.

when he cries. If you give in and take him out when he cries, he will always cry at night until you take him out.

Your puppy's crate is his home. When you have to leave your puppy in the house alone, leave him in his crate. Then take him out to his bathroom spot as soon as you get home. If someone is always watching your puppy, you will be able to housebreak him very fast. After a few days he will feel very safe in his crate and will not cry. When you have to travel or take him to the vet, you can take him in his crate and he will be easier to handle.

TAKE CARE OF YOUR PUPPY

When your dog is just a pup, he does not need a bath. A good brush will keep his coat clean and neat. If your pup has to have a bath because he is too messy, be sure that mom uses only soap meant for puppies and be sure to get all the soap out of his coat. If it is cold, use a blow dryer to dry him right away. If not, he can catch a chill and get sick.

Whenever you give your puppy a bath, he will first have to have his coat brushed out. If he has matted hair, the mats will not go away when you bathe him. They will get worse. Brush his hair so that you can see down to the skin. Make him stand as still as he can while you brush. You can also hold his feet for a few minutes to get him used to having his

Make sure mom helps you when it's time to give your puppy his first bath. Dogs don't need baths as often as you do. And they don't like them much either.

nails clipped. Talk to him all the time to let him know you are happy with him.

If he is the type of dog that will have to go to a grooming shop, be sure to take him when he is young. If you take him when he is young, he will not be afraid to go. If you wait until he is older, he may be afraid and will not like to get groomed.

You may think that since your puppy does not have very much hair he does not need to be brushed as often. That is wrong, because the brushing makes his skin healthy and teaches him to be still for future brushings.

There are different kinds of brushes for different kinds of dogs. Talk to your pet shop owner and find out the best kind for your type of dog.

Check your dog for fleas and ticks. Fleas are very small and hard to see but they run around on your dog. You can find them easiest on your dog's tummy when he lies on his back. The fleas can jump off your dog and onto your furniture. Flea powder is easy to use if you need it. Ticks are easier to see. Sometimes they look like warts on your dog's skin. Spray tick spray, which is sold in pet shops, directly on the ticks, which then die and soon fall off. These powders and sprays come in different concentrations, be sure to get the one that is right for your dog or puppy.

Some owners like to use flea and tick collars on their dogs. Your dog might be sensitive to such a collar and it can make his skin sore. Check with your vet about a collar for your dog.

Teach your puppy to stand on a grooming table. Show-dog puppies can learn this fast.

Watch carefully when you brush your dog. Sometimes you may see a flea or a tick. This Collie has a clean and pretty coat.

When you take care of your dog by brushing it, you can check for skin problems, fleas, and ticks.

You should also watch your puppy for signs of worms. There are different kinds of worms that your puppy might get. Your new puppy might vomit, have diarrhea, or have runny eyes or nose. Your vet needs to see this puppy right away.

All puppies should have shots that are used to protect them against certain diseases. The vet will give your puppy shots that will help keep him from getting sick.

Before you train your puppy to do anything, he should be healthy. A healthy puppy will eat well, will play and run, and will look happy. A sick puppy will not eat and may have a runny nose or eyes. He will not look like a happy, healthy puppy.

LESSONS TO BUILD ON

When you are training your puppy, always use a happy voice. Your puppy wants to make you happy, so when he does his lesson right say "Good boy" or "Good girl."

LESSON ONE: FEEDING TUFFY

Tuffy, as a puppy, needs a lot of sleep and he also needs to have puppy-size meals. He cannot eat very much at each meal, so three or four meals a day is better for him than one or two bigger ones.

When you give Tuffy his food, he may be very hungry. Tell Tuffy to sit before you give him his food. Say "Tuffy, sit." When you say "Sit," push down gently on his rear to show him how to sit. Do not push down hard and do not tell him to sit in a loud voice. Show him you love him. As soon as he sits down, say "Good dog." After Tuffy sits down, put the food down for him and say "Okay." This means that Tuffy can eat now. He should stand up and eat.

This lesson must be done every time you feed him. Always say the same thing so that he will learn the words "Tuffy, sit." Always say "Okay" to let Tuffy know that he can begin. Then pat Tuffy or rub his neck and say "Good dog" or "Good boy."

While Tuffy is still a puppy this lesson may take a long time to learn. Do not get angry at him when he does not sit. Repeat "Tuffy, sit" and push down on his rear. As soon as he is sitting, say "Good boy" and give him his food. Soon he will learn that he must sit before he gets his food. He will also learn the word "sit."

This lesson is a very good one for your puppy to learn. He will learn not to jump up on you when you are bringing his meal; he will sit so that he can have his food.

Your pet will learn his lessons, but he needs to do the same lesson over and over to remember it. Remember that he is just a puppy and training takes time.

FACING PAGE:
Make your dog sit by pushing lightly on his rear. Once he is sitting, say "Good boy" and give him his food.

You can get your dog to come by scratching a stick on the ground. Remember to say "Come" and call your dog by name.

Review

1. When feeding Tuffy, tell Tuffy to sit. Say "Tuffy, sit." Push down on his rear at the same time you say "Sit."
2. Say "Good boy" and pat Tuffy or rub his neck.
3. Say "Okay" and give him his food.

LESSON TWO: COME WHEN CALLED

Your puppy will be looking for things to do. He will play with his puppy toys and will chew on his chew bone. Make sure that he has things to chew on to help his puppy teeth grow. Nylabone®, which is sold in most pet shops, is very good for this. Just like you lose your baby teeth, so does your puppy.

Your puppy might not feel very well at times and you need to know that when he feels sick, he might need a trip to the vet to find out why. You cannot train a sick puppy; he will not play or eat very well. If your puppy has runny eyes, a very dry or hot nose, he may need to see a vet.

When Tuffy is playing and you are going to feed him or play with him, call him to come to you. Say "Tuffy, come." He will learn to come to you when you say this. If you say too many words, he will not know what you mean.

When he comes to you, say "Good boy" and pat or rub his neck. Always rub his neck, because some puppies think you are going to hit them on the head when you go to pat them on the head. You do not want to make Tuffy afraid. If you do, he will not come to you.

While he is still young, Tuffy may not come to you when you say "Tuffy, come"; just say "Good boy" and catch him. When he is older, you will use a leash. While he is young, do the lesson over and over again and he will learn to come. When you call him to eat, he will come to you very

Always reward your puppy once he has come to you. All dogs love to be praised for doing good.

fast. Say "Good boy," so that he will know you are happy he came to you.

Show him lots of love and try not to get angry when Tuffy does not learn very fast. Some puppies learn very slowly. Just make sure you say the same words each time.

Even if you have a fenced yard, you should teach Tuffy to come to you. Hold a toy for him to play with and call him to you. He will want to play and will come to you. Say "Tuffy, come." Then give him the toy and say "Good boy."

When you play with your puppy, you can have fun throwing a ball for him to chase or to bring back to you. You can toss a stick for him to pick up. Always think about your puppy as a grown dog. If you play with your puppy and let him jump on you, that is what he will do when he is older and bigger. If you let him pull on your clothes, he might pull on someone else's clothes. Dogs do not know which is a good shoe or which is an old shoe that they can chew. Puppies and dogs should *never* chew shoes—give them doggie chew toys like Gumabone® or Nylabone®.

Do not let your puppy bite on your fingers or snap at you, even when he is playing. Hold your puppy's mouth closed with one hand and slap your wrist to make a loud noise. Say "No!" when he tries to bite. Then give him a toy that he can chew. Puppies need to know that they do not bite people–only food and chew toys.

Your puppy will come when you call him to eat or to play . Make play time a happy time for Tuffy and he will come to you when you say "Tuffy, come."

Review

1. Call Tuffy to play or eat. Say "Tuffy, come." You can show him a toy or his food.

2. When Tuffy comes to you say "Good boy" and rub his neck.

LESSON THREE: THE LEASH AND COLLAR

When Tuffy is older (six months old), you will want to take him for walks. You will need to buy a collar and leash. A leather or nylon collar is a good collar for him to wear in the house or yard. While he is still growing, you need to check the collar to make sure it is not too tight. You should be able to fit two fingers under the collar to make sure your puppy can breathe.

When you are training him, you will use a training collar. Some people call a training collar a "choke chain." The training collar will not choke your dog if you use it right. You can start to use a training collar to train Tuffy when he is six months old. When you start the lessons with the training collar, you will need to do it every day for 15–30 minutes. A

Never squeeze your dog too hard, even if he is a very good boy!

A collar should never be tight on a puppy. Remember he is growing every day and so check it every day.

short lesson every day is better than a long lesson one time a week. Your puppy needs to hear the same words and do the same lesson over and over to learn.

The training collar is only for his lesson times. Do not leave the training collar on Tuffy when he is in the house or yard. It might get caught on something and hurt him.

Each lesson will take at least one week for Tuffy to learn. If he does not learn the lesson in one week, stay with the lesson until he learns what you want him to do. At the end of the week you can show your family the new lesson Tuffy has learned.

The important thing to remember when you are teaching your dog these lessons is not to get angry with him. You are the teacher and if your puppy is not learning the lesson, then you may not be teaching it right. If you are angry with your puppy, he will not be happy, and he cannot learn his lessons when he is not happy. Training time should be a happy time for both of you.

The first part of this lesson is for you. You must learn to put the training collar on Tuffy in the right way so it will not choke him. The training collar should slide back and forth very easily when you pull on it. The collar should have at least one inch of chain past the circle when it is on Tuffy.

The loose end that goes to the leash is on the left side when you are facing him. If the training collar is not on correctly, it will slide up to his neck and stay tight. You want the collar to slide back down to the circle very easily.

Be sure that the collar and leash are the right size for the type of dog that you have. If you have a small dog, the chain and leash should also be small.

Review

1. Buy a training collar and leash for training your dog when he is six months old. That is the best time to start. However, you can start training your dog any time after he's six months old.

2. The training collar should have at least one inch of extra chain. Be sure the size is right for your dog.

3. Learn to put the training collar on so that it will not hurt your dog. It should slide easily.

4. Begin the lessons and do them every day for at least 15 minutes.

Good dogs walk on leads without pulling. This Jack Russell Terrier likes walking on a leash.

LESSON FOUR: WALKING ON A LEASH

When you start dog training lessons, try to do them at times when Tuffy will want to learn. If he has been playing, he may not feel like learning his lessons. You are the teacher and you want Tuffy to learn. If you have a place to keep Tuffy for a half hour before his lessons, he will be so happy to get out that he will like his lessons. This place can be a laundry room, travel cage, or even a bathroom.

Bring Tuffy out and take off his leather or nylon collar. Put his training collar on him the correct way. Attach the leash, and you are ready for lesson four. Try to make sure that Tuffy knows that it is lesson time and not play time. Be sure to rub his neck and tell him "Good boy."

You want to make the lesson time a fun time for you and Tuffy. If you feel like you are getting too angry at him, stop the lesson and continue it later that same day. Always do the lesson each day. That is the only way he will learn.

For all of the lessons, take Tuffy to a place where you can walk around and not bump into things like trees or flowers. The ground should be easy to walk on and not have holes to fall into. Be sure to wear shoes that will not fall off or slip easily. Do not wear things that make a lot of noise when you walk. You want Tuffy to hear you and not watch other things going on around him.

During the first few weeks of lessons, stay away from other dogs

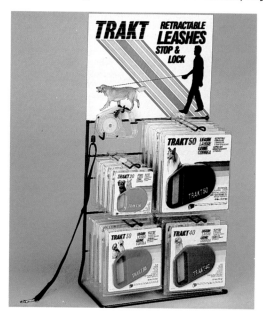

Since you'll be walking your dog every day, leash training is very important. Once he is well trained to walk on the leash, you can try a retractable leash which allows your dog to go a little farther and gives him more freedom. Photo courtesy Rolf C. Hagen.

Never train your dog where there are a lot of distractions. These flowers are more fun and smell better than you do. Remember that puppies cannot think about too many things at once.

and children. Later you might have other people and other dogs around, but for now Tuffy needs to listen to only you.

When you train Tuffy, he will always be on your *left* side. You will hold the leash in your *right* hand. Hold the leash so that your hand is at your waist. Your left hand will hang straight down. There should always be a loose leash hanging down to your dog. The leash should make a "J" type of figure to the collar. This way the training collar will never be too tight for Tuffy.

When you are teaching Tuffy his lessons, he will not always do what you want him to do. That is when you use the training collar to show him he is wrong. There is only one way to show him. Since you do not want to hurt Tuffy, you do not ever hit or kick him. You train him with the collar *only*. You pull the leash quickly, and then let it go quickly. The snap of the collar will say to Tuffy that his neck gets pinched if he does not do the lesson right. The training collar will loosen and slide back down to the "J." You must always have a loose leash so that Tuffy will learn that when he does the right thing the collar will feel good. You cannot drag Tuffy around for his lessons. The collar can only work right if you have a "J" loop down to his collar. When you pull the leash to tell him he is wrong, use your left hand on the leash. Then put it back down to your side.

If the dog is bigger than you, make sure mom comes along on the walk.

Now you are ready to do the first leash training lesson. You have put Tuffy in his waiting place for a half hour; you have put the training collar on correctly; you have a leash on the collar and the leash is in your right hand.

You are going to teach Tuffy to heel and to sit. The word "heel" means that Tuffy is walking at your left side with his head at your left knee. The word "sit" means that Tuffy is sitting at your left side with his head at your left knee. You are both facing forward, ready to go.

When you start this lesson, Tuffy will not know what you want him to do at first. You must show Tuffy what you want. When you start, tell Tuffy to sit at your left side. Say "Tuffy, sit" and push down on his rear to show him how to do it. As soon as he sits, rub his neck and say "Good boy." Then say "Tuffy, heel" and step forward with your *left* foot. Always step with your left foot first when you want Tuffy to come with you. The

left leg is the "go" leg. Tuffy is sitting by your left side, so when he sees your left leg move, that means that he moves too. When you stop and say "Sit," your left leg moves last. That tells Tuffy to stop, because he watches your left leg. Say "Sit" and push on his rear at the same time.

Always do this lesson the same way and soon Tuffy will get the idea. Do not get angry but be firm. Do these steps:

1. Start with Tuffy sitting at your left side.

2. Say "Tuffy, heel," then step with your left foot and walk straight to another spot (about ten steps away).

3. Stop with your left foot moving last and say "Sit" and push on his rear at the same time.

4. Say "Good boy" and rub his neck. Do not move to be by Tuffy's side. Move Tuffy to be by *your* side.

When you are walking, do not drag Tuffy by the leash. If he does not keep up with you, give the leash a snap and let go. If he is doing what you want him to do, say "Good boy" while you are walking. Each time you stop and tell Tuffy to sit, say "Good boy" and rub his neck to show him how

A Sheltie puppy getting used to his collar and leash.

well he is doing.

At the end of the lesson time, say "Okay" and play a little with Tuffy, keeping the collar and leash on him. When you do this, he will learn that as soon as the lesson is over he cannot run off and play.

After the first week of training, you do not need to put him in a waiting place for a half hour before his lessons. He will want to do his training because it is a fun time. He wants to make you happy, so always show Tuffy what you want him to do without getting angry.

Taking a rest for the camera.

Play with your dog while he's still on the lead. This makes him happy to be with you and he won't mind the leash at all!

Review

1. Put the training collar and leash on in the correct way. There will always be a "J" shape to the leash down to the collar. That way you know there is enough room so that the collar will not pinch his neck.

2. Tuffy will always be on your left side.

3. The left leg is the "go" leg. Always step off with your left leg first when you want Tuffy to go with you.

4. Hold the leash in your right hand with your left hand straight down. Your right hand will be at your waist.

5. When you are showing Tuffy that he is wrong, pull the leash fast and let go fast. Use your left hand to pull. That will pinch his neck to tell him he is wrong.

6. At the end of the lesson time, say "Okay" and play with him.

7. Do not take the leash and collar off right away; wait a few minutes and then take it off.

LESSON FIVE: HEEL AND SIT

This week you will not need to say "Sit" when you stop. Tuffy will know that when you stop he must sit right away. If he does not sit when you stop, snap the leash and push on his rear to show him. Do not say "Sit." Tuffy knows that when you stop, he sits.

Your dog will stop and sit when you stop. When you're ready to go again, he will get up and follow.

Walk around the training area with Tuffy; walk slowly and then quickly. Do not change speeds fast. Tuffy will learn to keep up with you. You are the teacher, so show Tuffy where you want him to walk. Be in charge. Start making turns and circles when you are walking. Tuffy must learn to walk with you everywhere you go. You can walk around poles or garbage cans for practice.

This week you can walk and stop and Tuffy will heel at your left side. If Tuffy walks too fast, snap his collar to show him he is wrong. If you pull on his collar slowly you will be in a tug-of-war with him. When you pull very fast and let go quickly, he will know that he should stay by your side. When you stop, Tuffy will sit right away. If he is not doing this, then you should make him sit sooner by snapping the collar with a fast pull on the lead.

Do not take the leash off his collar when you are working with him. Later he will walk by your side without the leash. This week only make him feel good about walking by your side and sitting when you stop.

LESSONS TO BUILD ON

Review

    1. Say "Tuffy, heel" and walk with your left foot first.

    2. Stop and Tuffy should sit without your having to say "Sit."

    3. Always rub his neck and say "Good boy" when he sits.

    4. Make sure Tuffy is heeling by your left side and not pulling on the leash.

This Bearded Collie would rather hug than tug!

LESSON SIX: STAY

    This week you will show Tuffy, with his collar and leash on, how to "stay" in one place.

    After you have walked around with Tuffy a little and you have stopped, he will be sitting. Use your left hand and hold it in front of his nose. Do not hold it too close to his nose or he will think you are going to hit him. At the same time, say "Stay." If you say the word slowly, Tuffy will know that the word means sit still.

    Take one step forward with your *right* foot. Remember that the left foot is the "go" foot when you want Tuffy to follow you. The right foot

is the "stay" foot. Tuffy is now trained to follow your left foot. If you step with your right foot first, Tuffy will know that he is not to follow you. The right foot is the "stay" foot because it is away from Tuffy and he does not see it move first when you tell him to stay.

Take one step and turn toward Tuffy. If he tries to move with you, step back and snap the leash to show him that he must stay. Say "Stay" again.

Once he sits, hold your left hand in front of his nose and say "Stay."

Do this:

1. Walk with Tuffy, say "Tuffy, heel," then stop. Tuffy will sit. Hold your left hand in front of his nose and say "Stay" in a normal, calm voice. Hold the leash tighter to make him stay.

2. Take a step with your *right* foot and stand in front of Tuffy. After you tell him to stay, drop your hand back down at your side. Stand in front of him for only a minute and then step back to his side and say "Good boy." If he moves, push his rear down to make him sit in the same place you left him.

Since 1952, Tropical Fish Hobbyist has been the source of accurate, up-to-the-minute, and fascinating information on every facet of the aquarium hobby. Join the more than 60,000 devoted readers worldwide who wouldn't miss a single issue.

Subscribe right now so you don't miss a single copy!

Return To:
Tropical Fish Hobbyist, P.O. Box 427, Neptune, NJ 07753-0427

YES! Please enter my subscription to *Tropical Fish Hobbyist*. Payment for the length I've selected is enclosed. U.S. funds only.

CHECK ONE:
- ❏ 1 year-$40 — 12 ISSUES
- ❏ 2 years-$75 — 24 ISSUES
- ❏ 3 years-$100 — 36 ISSUES
- ❏ 5 years-$160 — 60 ISSUES

(Please allow 4-6 weeks for your subscription to start.) *Prices subject to change without notice*

❏ LIFETIME SUBSCRIPTION (max. 30 Years) $695.
❏ SAMPLE ISSUE $4.50
❏ GIFT SUBSCRIPTION. Please send a card announcing this gift. I would like the card to read: _____
❏ I don't want to subscribe right now, but I'd like to have one of your FREE catalogs listing books about pets. Please send catalog to:

SHIP TO:
Name _____
Street _____ Apt. No. _____
City _____ State _____ Zip _____

U.S. Funds Only. Canada and Mexico add $11.00 per year; Foreign add $20.00.

Charge my: ❏ VISA ❏ MASTER CHARGE ❏ PAYMENT ENCLOSED

_____
Card Number   Expiration Date

_____
Cardholder's Name (if different from "Ship to:")

_____
Cardholder's Address (if different from "Ship To:")

_____
Cardholder's Signature

SM 402

BRAND NEW: The Best Herp Magazine in the Business!

REPTILE
H O B B Y I S T

CARPET
PYTHONS

Ribbon Snakes
Frilled Dragons
Emerald Swifts

ISSN 0041-3259

***Reptile Hobbyist* is the source for accurate, up-to-the-minute, practical information on *every* facet of the herpetological hobby. Join many thousands of devoted readers worldwide who wouldn't miss a single valuable issue.**

Subscribe right now so you don't miss a single copy!

Return To:

Reptile Hobbyist, P.O. Box 427, Neptune, NJ 07753-0427

YES! Please enter my subscription to *Reptile Hobbyist*. Payment for the length I've selected is enclosed. U.S. funds only.

CHECK ONE: ❏ 6 issues-$20 ❏ 12 issues-$38 ❏ 18 issues-$50 ❏ 30 issues-$80

(Please allow 4-6 weeks for your subscription to start.) *Prices subject to change without notice*

❏ SAMPLE ISSUE $4.50

❏ GIFT SUBSCRIPTION. Please send a card announcing this gift.
I would like the card to read: _____

❏ I don't want to subscribe right now, but I'd like to have one of your FREE catalogs listing books about pets. Please send catalog to:

SHIP TO:

Name _____

Street _____ Apt. No. _____

City _____ State _____ Zip _____

U.S. Funds Only. Canada and Mexico add $6.00 per year; Foreign add $10.00.

Charge my: ❏ VISA ❏ MASTER CHARGE ❏ PAYMENT ENCLOSED

_____

Card Number   Expiration Date

_____

Cardholder's Name (if different from "Ship to:")

_____

Cardholder's Address (if different from "Ship To:")

_____

Cardholder's Signature

SM 402

Training is serious business. Some dogs pay attention better than others.

Do more heeling and then do the "stay" lesson again. Do not move very far away from Tuffy when you put him in his "sit, stay"; you might need to step back and push his rear down to show him not to move.

After a few days of standing in front of Tuffy for the lesson, you can take two steps in front of Tuffy. When you step away with your right foot, do not back away from Tuffy. Your left hand is in front of his nose and you are facing forward. You then step forward with your right foot and face Tuffy when you turn around. Do not go to the end of the leash until Tuffy will stay when you take one step.

After you step back to Tuffy, rub his neck and say "Good boy." Then you can walk around heeling with him for a while before the lesson is over.

Review

1. Show Tuffy how to stay: Hold your left hand in front of his nose. Say "Stay" in a slow voice. Hold the leash tighter, holding him back.

2. Step with your right foot forward one step and turn to face Tuffy.

3. After one minute, step back to his side and say "Good boy."

4. Later in the week, take two steps away from him. Soon you will be able to walk to the end of the leash. Remember: Do not step very far away from Tuffy until he learns to stay. As soon as he moves, show him "stay" all over again.

Teach "stay" in the standing position too. Remember not to use your dog's name when practicing the "stay."

LESSON SEVEN: SIT, STAY AND A SHOW FINISH

This week you will work with Tuffy to make sure he will stay at all times. If you leave Tuffy alone outside a place that does not allow dogs, you want to be sure he is waiting there for you when you get back.

First you will need to be sure Tuffy will stay when you walk to the end of the leash. When he can do this very well, you can start this second part of the "stay" lesson.

Put Tuffy in the "sit, stay" command position. Walk to the end of the leash and turn around to face him. Do not say Tuffy's name at first

because he will think you want him to come to you. That lesson is later. Right now you want Tuffy to stay when you tell him to stay. Move around while still holding on to the leash. You can dance, or sing, or hop around. If Tuffy moves, you must move right back to his side and tell him with a snap of the collar to stay.

If Tuffy makes a mistake and moves, then start over with a "sit, stay" and take one step away from Tuffy to show him that this is the "sit, stay" lesson.

Start leaving him in the "sit, stay" for a longer time. Two or three minutes is good to start. You should always watch that he does not move. If he lies down, you need to move back to his side and make him sit up.

At the end of the week you can say Tuffy's name. Do not say it as if you were calling him. If he moves to come to you, put him back and say "Sit, stay" again.

When Tuffy knows how to sit and stay when you tell him, then you can go on to the hard part of this lesson. Tell Tuffy to "Stay" and lay the leash down in front of his nose. Step forward about three steps and turn around. When you face Tuffy, watch to make sure he does not move. You have to be fast if he decides to move. He should know that he must

You can remind your dog to stay by holding his shoulders for a brief moment.

stay when you tell him to stay, even if you are not holding the leash.

Do this lesson until you can move further away without Tuffy moving. Then do it for longer times. This is a hard lesson for some dogs. They think that you are going to leave them and they want to follow you. If Tuffy moves, you need to start the "sit, stay" lesson over until he learns the meaning of the word "stay."

When Tuffy will sit and stay even when you lay the leash down, you can do the show finish. This is the way to go back to your dog when you are in the show ring. If you decide to show your dog at a dog show that has an obedience trial, this is the right way to do the show finish.

The judge will tell you to put your dog in a "sit, stay" and leave your dog. After one minute he will say, "Return to your dog." You will walk to your dog and circle around on the right side to step to his right side. Then his right shoulder will be at your left knee.

When you are doing this at home, make sure that Tuffy does not move to see where you are going when you walk around behind him. When you are showing him this lesson, you can pick up the leash when you walk to him and then you will have it in your hand when you get back to his side. If he moves, snap the collar. He should stay until you are back by his side. He should stay even when you are moving all around him.

The show finish is a good thing to know, but if you are not going to show your dog you do not need to do this part of the stay lesson.

Showing your dog in an obedience trial is fun and a good way of training your dog to be around other dogs. When you can take your dog around a lot of other dogs in a dog show and he does what you want instead of running off to play, you are a good dog trainer.

Review

1. Put Tuffy in a "sit, stay." Walk to the end of the leash and turn to face him.

2. After Tuffy will stay for three minutes with the leash on, you can lay his leash in front of him. When you leave him, walk a little further than the leash and turn to face him.

3. Make sure you can move back to him very fast if he tries to move. You need to snap his collar if he moves.

4. Start saying his name and moving around while he is staying. Don't call him to you, just say his name so he will know that he is not to come until you say "Come."

5. If you want to show finish, you will put him on "sit, stay" and step off with your right foot and leave him. To return to him you will walk around his back and end up with his right shoulder at your left knee in the heeling position. When you are facing him, you will walk to the right and

walk around behind him. He must be still when you do this. If he is not still, use the collar to show him to stay.

LESSON EIGHT: COME FROM THE STAY

Tuffy learned the word "come" when he was a puppy, so this

Use the leash to cue your dog to "come" once he has sat down and stayed for you.

lesson will be easy for him to learn.

When he is sitting, say "Stay" and use the hand signal in front of his nose. Step off with the right foot and go to the end of the leash and face him. Say "Tuffy, come" and pull the leash at the same time. Run backwards a few steps and stop. When you stop, push Tuffy's rear down so he will sit in front of you. Say "Good boy" and rub his neck. Tuffy will learn to come and sit in front of you when you call him.

You do not want Tuffy to forget his "stay" lesson, so if Tuffy comes to you before you tell him to come, start this part over. Do some heeling and then say "Stay." Then do heeling and stopping again. Make sure that Tuffy is learning the words and what each one means. When you say "Come" in a happy voice, he will come to you. If you say "Stay" in a slow

Entering your dog in an outdoor dog show will be a good test of your training. There are many distractions and things to see at dog shows.

voice, he knows that he should not move. In all the lessons you will see that when you want Tuffy to do something that means for him to move, you always say "Tuffy" first. That will make him watch and listen for you to tell him what to do. When you want him to be still, you only say the word. You will always say "Tuffy, heel," "Tuffy, come," but you will only say "Sit" or "Stay." In all of the moving lessons you will say his name first. So for "come" you will say "Tuffy, come."

When you were doing the "sit, stay" lesson you left Tuffy and went to the end of the leash. You said his name and he did not come to you. He should not come to you when you say only his name. You must say "Come" before he comes to you.

After Tuffy learns the word "come" and he comes and sits in front of you, you do not need to pull the leash. When Tuffy will stay and come to sit in front of you, it is time to use a long line such as a nylon lead or long cord on a spool. It will be much longer and you can train Tuffy to come and sit in front of you when you walk further away.

To do the show finish on the "come" of the "recall," as it is called in an obedience trial, do this: Leave Tuffy in a "sit, stay." Go to the end of the leash and call Tuffy to sit in front of you. Say "Tuffy, come." When he is sitting in front of you close enough for you to reach out and touch his nose, the judge will tell you to finish. To teach him this lesson, you will first pull him around your right side to sit at your left knee. You say "Tuffy, heel." If you take two or three steps backwards and pull him around you when you say "Tuffy, heel," he will get the idea that he should walk around you and sit at your left knee. It is almost the same as when you left Tuffy on a "sit, stay" and then went back to him and around his back to stand at his side. Now he will do the same for the show finish at the recall but he will sit by your side.

When you do this lesson, do not turn around with your dog. You are standing still and facing forward. Only your

Even if your dog isn't doing well, never stop praising him. Training must always be fun for the dog.

dog walks around. Be sure to say "Good boy" at the end of the lesson. Tuffy needs to know that he is doing the right thing to make you happy.

Review

1. Tell Tuffy to stay.

2. Go to the end of the leash and face him.

3. Pull the leash and run backwards a few steps and say "Tuffy, come" in a happy voice.

4. Tuffy will stop in front of you. Push his rear to show him to sit in front of you when he comes to you.

5. After he learns to run to you when you say "Come," you do not need to run backwards.

6. You can use a light line that is longer than his leash. Tie it to his collar and put Tuffy in a "sit, stay." Go to the end of the long line and say "Tuffy, come."

7. When he comes to you, he will sit in front of you.

8. Show finish: Say "Tuffy, heel" and pull him around to sit at your left knee while you are taking two or three steps backwards. Later, when Tuffy gets the idea that he should walk to your left side and sit, you do not need to take the steps backwards.

9. When he is sitting by your left side, say "Good boy" and pat him.

At first you can teach your dog to lie down by lifting his left paw and pulling his leg so that he goes into the right position.

Make your dog stay "down" before you continue walking.

LESSON NINE: DOWN, STAY

This week you will show Tuffy how to lie down. When you do this lesson you must first show Tuffy what you mean. Stand with Tuffy on your left side. Bend down and hold his left paw with your left hand and pull his leg to lay him down at the same time you say "Down."

Do the heeling, staying and coming lessons and add the down lesson a few times. After Tuffy learns the word "down," you do not need to show him how to do it by pulling his leg to lay him down. Remember that this is a lesson for him to be still, so you do not say his name first. In all the lessons that are moving lessons, you say "Tuffy, come" or "Tuffy, heel." For the stay lessons you only say "Stay," not "Tuffy, stay." So for the down lesson you only say "Down."

When you tell Tuffy "Down," he should now lie down. If he does not lie when you say "down," step gently on the "J" loop of the collar; this will pull his head down to the ground. Say "Good boy" as soon as he is down and then let him up. Soon he will learn that when you say "Down" he should lie down right away.

When Tuffy will lie down when you tell him to, he is ready for the next part of the down lesson.

When you are heeling and stop, Tuffy will be sitting by your left side. Say "Down" and Tuffy will lie down. Say "Stay" with your left hand in front of his nose. This is just like the "sit, stay" lesson, but now Tuffy is lying down. Tell him to stay and take a step in front of him, stepping off with your right leg (the "stop" leg). Do not back away from him. After a minute, step back to his side and say "Tuffy, heel" and take two steps.

Always take two steps before you tell him "Good boy" for lying down. If you try to pat him when he is lying down, he will sit up. If you walk back to him and he sits up or moves, snap the leash and say "Down" again. You must teach him to stay down until you say "Heel." He should not get up when you say "Tuffy." You can wait a few seconds before you say the second half just to make sure he moves only when you say "Heel." Say "Tuffy . . . heel." Then move the two steps and stop with Tuffy sitting at your left side. Then you say "Good boy" and rub his neck.

Showing the dog the palm of your hand means "stay."

This lesson also has a show finish. When you leave Tuffy on a "down, stay" and he will stay a few minutes, you can start to do the show finish. In the obedience trial, Tuffy must be able to stay down in the same place for three minutes. Then you will walk back to him and around his right side to stand with his head at your left knee. Then the judge will say to you that the "Exercise is finished," which tells you that you can say "Tuffy, heel" and take two steps forward to make Tuffy sit at your left side. Say "Good boy" and rub his neck. If Tuffy can lie still for three minutes with other dogs near him, he will be a very well-trained dog. Sometimes another dog will not be very nice and will get up and come over to Tuffy in the obedience trial. That is a real test for Tuffy–when he will lie down and stay with a strange dog sniffing at him.

Review

1. Show Tuffy how to lie down. Stand beside him and hold his left paw with your left hand. Pull the leg until he is lying down.

2. When Tuffy will lie down when you say "Down," add the "stay" just like you did with the "sit, stay." Put your left hand in front of his nose and take a step forward with your right foot. Turn and face him. After a minute, step back to him and say "Heel" and take two steps forward. Then say "Good boy" and rub his neck. Be sure to snap the leash and step back to his side if he moves or gets up.

3. When you do a show finish, you walk around to the right and go back to stand at Tuffy's other side, putting him at the place where he

Only a gentle well-behaved puppy, like this Australian Shepherd, will let you carry him like this.

will be in at the heel position. Then take two steps forward and Tuffy will sit at your left knee. Say "Good boy" and rub his neck.

LESSON TEN: LESSONS WITHOUT A LEASH

By this time your friend Tuffy has learned to sit, stay, heel, lie down, come, and down-stay. Your dog has good manners and should make you happy.

Now you can teach him to do his lessons without the leash on him. It is a good lesson to teach Tuffy because he must do what you tell him to do, even if he does not have his leash on. You may some day save his life if he runs in front of a car. You can say "Tuffy, come" and Tuffy will come to you.

You can say "Down" if Tuffy wants to jump up or if you have him in the house. And now you can say "Tuffy, heel" when you want to go for

Before starting a lesson without a leash, calm your dog down and make him feel happy about beginning a new lesson. He doesn't have to know that this lesson is harder than all the others.

Practice stacking your dog at home whenever you have the chance. This Shar-Pei will be good and ready for the show ring.

a walk in the country.

All of the lessons that Tuffy has learned can be done without a leash. Tie a long training leash (15 feet) to his training collar with the six-foot leash also on. Do the heel lesson for a while. Say "Stay" after he sits down. Take the six-foot leash off the collar and lay it down in front of you. He will have only the light line on his collar. Tuffy will know that the leash is off his collar. Do the heel lesson again. Tuffy will think that he does not have a leash on his collar and he might try to run off and play. If he does, do not say anything. Hold on to the light line tightly. When he comes to the end of the long line, Tuffy will pinch his own neck. Make sure that he comes back to you, and do the heeling lesson again. He will soon learn that he must heel even when his leash is off. After he learns the heel lesson using only the light line, you can go on to do the stay and come lessons with the light line. When Tuffy will do each lesson with the light line, you can take the light line off for a few minutes. This is the time you might need to have a short piece of cloth or leather tied to the loop on his training collar where the leash is hooked. If you have to snap his collar to tell him he is wrong, you need to have something to hold onto to snap the collar.

Review

1. Use a long light leash.

2. Tie it to the training collar with the leash on his collar at the same time.

3. After heeling for a while, say "Stay" and take the leash off and lay it down so Tuffy can see that it is not on his collar.

4. Hold the light line and say "Tuffy, heel." Heel with the light line.

5. If Tuffy tries to run off, or does the lesson wrong, use the light line to make him do it right.

6. Start out using the light line for only a few minutes and then put the leash back on his collar.

7. When you take the light line off after he is doing his lessons very well, tie a small piece of cloth or leather to the loop where his leash

Teaching your dog to stay will help lots when you're visiting the veterinarian together. A good dog will stand or sit quietly so that the vet can check him over.

A well-trained dog will behave when groomed and will stand still on the table. Look how blue the Chow Chow's tongue is!

is usually hooked. Use the cloth to snap his collar when he does not have a light line or leash hooked to it.

LESSON ELEVEN: STAND

A good thing for Tuffy to learn is how to "stand." This lesson is like the "sit, stay," only Tuffy will be standing and staying. This lesson is good if you have to take Tuffy to the vet and he needs to stand still or if you want to show Tuffy at a dog show.

This smart Old English Sheepdog shows off his "stand" for the judge.

This is also used in the obedience trial. The judge will pat his head and touch him lightly on the back and rear and Tuffy must stand still.

To teach this lesson to Tuffy, tell him to heel (when you come to a stop, Tuffy usually sits); you do not want him to sit, so say "Stand" and put your left hand under his belly to keep him from sitting. You can say "Good boy" and rub his neck to show him that it is okay to stand when you stop. After he learns that the word "stand" means to stay standing when you stop, you can say "Stay" and walk to the end of the leash.

When Tuffy has learned to "stand, stay" you can ask a friend or someone in your family to touch Tuffy on the head and back. A show judge will want to see your dog's teeth. Have your friend gently lift Tuffy's lips to check his bite. Tuffy should let people touch his mouth. Make sure you are near enough to snap his collar if he moves. He must stand very still and let the person walk around him. This is a very good test for Tuffy. Even if you want Tuffy to be a good watchdog, it is very good for him to learn to be still when you tell him to.

Review

1. Say "Tuffy, heel" and do some heeling around. When you are ready to stop, say "Stand" and put your hand under his belly to show him

how to stand.

2. If Tuffy tries to sit down, remember that he is only doing what you have trained him to do. Do not get angry. Show him how to stand every time he tries to sit.

3. When he knows how to stand you can say "Stay" and take one step away and face him. You can step further away after he has learned that he must stand still when you walk away from him.

4. Ask a friend to touch him on the head and rear. Tuffy should not move.

5. Later you can do a show finish and walk around Tuffy, ending

Begging is a trick that lots of dogs learn without being taught.

up with his head at your left knee. This is just like the sit and down show finish, only Tuffy is standing still.

LESSON TWELVE: THE TRICKSTER

This lesson will show you how to train your dog to do dog tricks just for fun. Tuffy likes to make you laugh and be happy. When he does these tricks, you and your friends will laugh.

When you train your dog to do a trick, keep in mind the kind of dog that you have. Terriers and Poodles are usually the best trick dogs

Here's the team taking a break from training. Dogs love to spend quiet time with their keepers.

because of their shorter bodies. If you own a Dachshund, it might be hard to teach him to sit up and beg because of his long body. A Great Dane looks odd when he sits up and begs because he is so big. A Bulldog is built with most of his weight in front and cannot usually learn to stand on his hind feet. Only do the tricks with your dog that he can learn to do.

Remember that when your dog learns a trick, he will do the trick even when you don't want him to do it. A "sit up and beg" might look cute in the yard but would annoy everyone at the dinner table. A "feet on the shoulder" trick for a Great Dane shows how gentle they are but your Great Dane might do it to someone who is afraid of dogs.

After the obedience training, these tricks are easy to teach. Any dog can learn to "play dead." Use only one or two words to teach the tricks. Your dog will know many words by now. Keep it easy.

Play Dead

This trick is the easiest to show a dog. Put Tuffy in a "down." Say "Down" and with a happy voice say "Play dead." At the same time roll him over with your hand onto his back and pull one leg at the same time to make him lie flat. As soon as he is flat on his side, say "Good boy" and let him up. When he gets the idea that "Play dead" means to lie on his side, you can let him do it for a longer period of time. Soon you can say "Play dead" without first saying "Down."

"Roll over" is a fun command to teach your dog. This sheepdog is enjoying his roll in the grass.

Sit Up and Beg

When you do this trick you can have a treat in your hand. Dog biscuits are good treats for dogs. Hold the treat behind you so your dog cannot see the biscuit. Tell your dog to "Sit, stay." At first, stand by your dog and say "Beg" in a happy voice. When you say "Beg," slide your right hand behind his front feet under his chest and hold him to a sit up. Make sure his back feet are under him with his toes and heels on the floor. He will balance on his heels and rear. Some dogs learn this faster than others, so take your time. As soon as he is up, say "Good boy," give him a treat, and let him down. Some dogs will wave their front feet after they have learned this lesson.

Roll Over

You can train your dog with a treat or just with a wave of your hand for this trick. I always like to train a dog with no treat. You want him to learn the lesson because it makes you happy. Some day you might not have a treat in your hand and Tuffy will be sad. Try this lesson like this: Tell Tuffy to lie down. When he is down say "Roll over" in a happy voice. At the same time hold his two front feet in your left hand. If Tuffy is lying down on his side with his front feet to the right, roll him over by taking his feet from the right over to the left. Your right hand should be in front of his eyes. Wave your hand around in a circle to show Tuffy which way to roll. As soon as you roll him over, say "Good boy" and let him up. After you do this a few times, Tuffy will learn to do the roll over from a sit.

After your dog has learned all his lessons, you will have a very special pet. When he does his lessons and minds his manners he will make everyone happy. You should be proud to have such a wonderful pet. You might have to show your dog a lesson over again to remind him later. Don't get angry. Dogs need to do all these lessons over and over again to remember them.

If you have someone to give you a test on each of these lessons, it will help your dog to learn to do them around other people.

FACING PAGE:
If your dog does the trick you want, be sure to reward him with praise and a treat too. This agile Sheltie is jumping for a dumbbell.

After you have worked with your dog to teach him good manners, you will be proud of him. You may want to take him to a dog show and win ribbons. Sometimes prizes are given in dog shows. Most of all it will be fun for you and your dog.

DOG SHOWS AND JUNIOR SHOWMANSHIP

There are many kinds of dog clubs to join. Some clubs help you to teach your dog to be around other dogs. He can learn to obey you when there is noise and movement around him. Remember to be a good dog owner by not letting your dog jump on other dogs or people. If they do not know your dog, they might worry that he will bite them.

If your dog is an "all-American" dog and not a purebred, you can show him in 4-H dog shows, fun matches, and city recreation dog shows.

The fun matches have classes that any dog will fit: smallest dog in the show, largest dog in the show, costume class that you can dress your dog in clothes or ribbons, and sometimes a trick class. Now that you have trained your dog to do tricks, he might win a prize. Even if you think your dog could not win a prize for his beauty, there may be a class for funniest looking, or even dogs that look like their masters.

The American Kennel Club (AKC) and the Kennel Club of England hold shows that can make your dog a champion. You can learn about showing your dog in the regular classes. He must be six months or older. A breed club will help you learn all about your purebred dog. Larger cities will usually have a club for every kind of purebred dog. They have fun matches to teach you about showing your dog.

Your dog should have his registration papers with your name or your parent's name listed on the registration. You can even show a relative's dog in Junior Showmanship. If the dog is owned by your uncle, aunt, grandmother, grandfather, or step-father or other step-family relation, you can show him. You can get all the rules by sending a letter to the AKC (American Kennel Club), 51 Madison Avenue, New York, New York 10010 or to The Kennel Club of Great Britain, 1 Clarges Street, Piccadilly, London W1Y 8AB.

The classes are novice junior class: For boys and girls who are at least 10 years old and under 13 years old on the day of the show and who,

Junior Showmanship can be a lot of fun for you and your dog. This Chow Chow and his handler have had a very special day together.

at the time entries close, have not won three first places in a novice class at a licensed or member show. Licensed show means that the national registry has given the okay for a club to give a show and award points that may make a dog a champion. The club must also obey all the rules of the major club.

Novice senior class: For boys and girls who are at least 13 years old and under 17 years old on the day of the show and who, at the time entries close, have not won three first places in a novice class at a licensed or member show.

Open junior class: For boys and girls who are at least 10 years old and under 13 years old on the day of the show and who, at the time entries close, have won three first places in a novice class at a licensed or member show.

Open senior class: For boys and girls who are at least 13 years old and under 17 years old on the day of the show and who, at the time entries close, have won three first places in a novice class at a licensed or member show.

"Entries close" means that your entry form must be mailed to the show superintendent before the date set, in order for them to make the show catalog that lists all the dogs in the show (usually two or three weeks).

A good reason for showing your dog in Junior Showmanship is to teach you how to show your dog in a way that will make him look his best. The judge is very helpful and after the judging will usually tell you what you should have done differently. This is a learning time for you and your dog. All types of dogs will be in the ring together and the better behaved your dog is, the better he will place in the ribbons. Try to visit a dog show

Always try to make your dog look as handsome as possible. This Bulldog is happy to be with such a good little handler.

Dog shows for kids can be great fun for you and your dog. You both can make new friends and learn about the sport of showing dogs.

before you enter one to see how it is done. You will see boys and girls with their well-mannered dogs waiting for the judging to begin. They will pick up an arm band that will tell the judge what number they are listed in the catalog. The arm band is put on the left arm above the elbow. The judge does not know your name or the name of your dog, so he must be able to see the number. When the time comes for the judging, the ring steward (a person who helps the judge) will call each number and line them up to get ready to go in the ring. The ring steward or the judge will tell the first person where to line up the dogs. If you are the first person to go in with your dog, you must listen to the judge or steward. There will have to be room behind you for the other dogs to line up. Do not push past another person to get in front of the line. Stay in the order that you are sent into the ring. After or during the judging, the judge may change your place in line.

You will then "stack" your dog. This is a way to stand your dog to make him look his best. You will go by the type of dog you own. Make sure your dog will not be disqualified so that he will not be sent out of the ring. If a dog cannot be shown in the regular classes or obedience classes, he cannot be shown in Junior Showmanship. All purebred dogs are supposed to look a certain way. A breed "standard" tells you how he should look. It's okay if Tuffy is not perfect, but he cannot have any really

Let's march in an American parade with this obedient American Staffordshire Terrier and his red, white and blue handler.

bad flaws.

When the judge tells you to "gait" your dog, or tells you to run down the ring and back, you should be able to trot your dog in a way that shows that he runs straight. This may take some time to train your dog to do. Be sure that he does not run sideways. You can help him run straight. Try to move forward as smoothly as you can. When you make a turn, practice doing it smoothly. You and your dog should practice many times before you do it for the judge in the ring. You can ask a friend or neighbor to be the "judge" and inspect your dog. He must stand still when the judge looks at him.

In the ring you must listen to the judge when he tells you where to gait. He may say "Do a figure 'L'" or "Make a triangle." You should move to that point and end up back at the judge. The judge wants to see that your dog has free movement. He can tell many things about your dog by seeing him move. You can help your dog look good by the way you lead him. Do not choke your dog when you run. You should train him at home

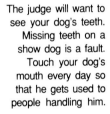

The judge will want to see your dog's teeth. Missing teeth on a show dog is a fault. Touch your dog's mouth every day so that he gets used to people handling him.

not to run with his head down. Make sure that he is ready to show before you go into the ring.

When the judge is looking at the other dogs, you can let your dog relax for a few moments. Do not make him stand stiff all the time but don't let him lie down or roll in the grass since the judge may not like this and the other dogs might get distracted. You will want him to enjoy being in a show. He will not like the show ring if he must stand like a rock at all times.

If you have done everything right and been a good sport, you will win like this handler and Siberian Husky.

You should be quiet so the judge can think about what he is doing. Do not talk to the other people in the ring or yell at their dogs.

You need to listen and pay attention to the judge. This will teach you to show your dog so that he looks his best.

When you are in the ring with many sizes of dogs, you must be careful that your dog does not run over the dog in front of you. If you have a very small dog, watch out that a big dog does not get so close to you that you will not show your dog very well or at his best gait.

The big dog needs to gait around at a faster pace. He can go around you when the judge tells everyone to go around the ring. Show good manners to the other dogs and people in the ring. They are doing their best.

If have a small dog that "shows" on a table for the judge, you should practice putting your dog on a table at home. He might get frightened on show day if he has never been set in a show stance on a table.

Since you have trained your dog at home by telling him he is a good dog with lots of pats, you do not need to give him treats in the show ring.

A dog as pretty as this Golden Retriever would be fun to handle in the show ring.

You may see people in the show rings that will give their dog a treat to make them look up, or show them a ball or toy to make them look at the handler, but this is not necessary. Just saying their name softly will do the same thing.

You might want to use a different type of leash to show your dog in Junior Showmanship. There are many different types of show leads. Different colors and sizes of leads are used and you might want to try one at home to make sure your dog will still have good manners when you use a different type of lead.

What you wear in the show ring is also important. The judge is looking at your dog, but he also looks at the way you present your dog. If you are dressed in sloppy clothes or strange patterns and colors, the judge's eye will go to you and your clothes and may not see how well you are showing your dog.

Think about the weather on the day of the dog show. You do not want to be too hot or too cold when you are trying to make your dog look his best.

Wear shoes that will not slip or fall off. If you have new shoes, be sure that you have worn them before so that you will not get blisters on your feet on show day.

Clothing color is not as important as how well your dog looks. You can wear light-colored clothing if you have a dark dog, or dark-colored clothing if you have a light-colored dog. But a costume is not a good idea. You should not have writing or pictures on your shirt telling your dog's name or showing his picture.

Be sure to learn all you can about your dog's standard, that is, the way your dog should look according to the rules of his own breed.

After the judge has asked the entire group to gait around, he will ask you each to gait in turn. Then he will look at your dog's teeth to make sure that he has the correct bite. He will look at his bite himself or ask you to show the dog's teeth to him. He will touch your dog over the back and, if it is a male dog, will check to see that your dog meets the standard for not being a cryptorchid. That means that your male dog's testicles must be fully descended.

If your male dog is going to be shown in dog shows, you must start him out in his training to stand still when the judge checks him. Sometimes male or female dogs will try to sit when the judge checks them. You can put your hand under the stomach to remind him to stand just like when you were training him.

If you have learned all that you can by watching dog shows or going to ring manner classes (given in most cities), you should do a very good job of showing your dog. Do not be afraid of making a mistake. Junior

Showmanship is for learning. Do not ask the judge questions while you are in the ring, or before the class. If he asks you a question, answer politely. Afterwards he may have time to talk to you and tell you what you could do better. Be a good winner or loser.

Most of all, have fun with your dog! Learn about showing your dog, and watch the people that know how to show your type of dog. There is a lot to learn, but with a well-mannered dog, you are off to a good start.

The smaller breeds, like the Chihuahua, must be shown on a table like this.

INDEX

SUGGESTED READING
—— FROM T.F.H. ——

Everybody Can Train Their Own Dog (TW-113)
The Essentials of Dog Training
Alphabetical and helpful.
Over 200 photos in full-color.

The Proper Care of Dogs (TW-102)
Care and buyer's guide by Christopher Burris.
More than 200 full-color photographs.

The Mini-Atlas of Dog Breeds (H-1106)
Lively survey of over 400 breeds with symbol captions by Andrew De Prisco and James B. Johnson.
Over 500 photos in color!